CW00371372

JIHAD, VIOLENCE, WAR AND PEACE IN ISLAM

by Tariq Ramadan

JIHAD, VIOLENCE, WAR AND PEACE IN ISLAM

by Tariq Ramadan

CLARITAS
BOOKS

1 2 3 4 5 6 7 8 9 10

CLARITAS BOOKS

Bernard Street, Swansea, United Kingdom
Milpitas, California, United States

CLARITAS
BOOKS

© CLARITAS BOOKS 2018

This book is in copyright. Subject to statutory exception and to the provisions
of relevant collective licensing agreements, no reproduction of any part may
take place without the written permission of
Claritas Books.

First Published in February 2017

Typeset in Garamond Pro 14/11

Jihad, Violence, War and Peace in Islam
by Tariq Ramadan
Translated by Myriam Francios

A CIP catalogue record for this book is available from the British Library

ISBN: 978-1-905837-39-7

TARIQ RAMADAN is Professor of Contemporary Islamic Studies at Oxford University. He is Senior Research Fellow at St Antony's College (Oxford) and Doshisha University (Kyoto, Japan); Visiting Professor at the Faculty of Islamic Studies, (Qatar); Director of the Research Centre of Islamic Legislation and Ethics (CILE) (Doha, Qatar) and President of the think tank European Muslim Network (EMN) in Brussels. His research interests include Islamic legislation, politics, ethics and Sufism. His writings include *In the Footsteps of the Prophet: Lessons from the Life of Muhammad*, *The Quest for Meaning: Developing a Philosophy of Pluralism* and *Radical Reform: Islamic Ethics and Liberation*.

CONTENTS

Introduction

Is the world of Islam intrinsically violent? What exactly does Islam say about violence? Is it legitimate, encouraged or, even, a commandment? The term 'jihad' which appears so frequently in the media, seems to encapsulate all the fears evoked by the mere mention of Islam and Muslims. Much has been written about 'holy war', of the mobilisation of fanatics and of the latest epidemic of rampant fundamentalism. As long as this 'gangrene of jihad' keeps hold its grip, the world of Islam will continue to terrorise the minds of many.

Therefore it seems that when one speaks of violence, one speaks of jihad. It is thus of primary importance to define and delineate the various facets of jihad. How is it that a concept so fundamental to Islam has come to represent one of its darkest characteristics? How has something which signifies such intense spirituality become one of the most negative symbols of religious expression? A reading of recent historical events carries its share of responsibility undoubtedly, but the distortion can be traced further back to the late Middle Ages.

The understanding of a certain number of Islamic concepts was restricted, very early on, to an exercise in mere comparison. During the time of the crusades there was Muslim expansion; since these were holy crusades, there must have been 'holy wars', and thus the infamous jihad. And while the West has thankfully overcome the primitive stage of holy wars, of crusades, one is bound to notice that today the Muslim world is lagging far behind, since we continue to observe groups, movements, parties and governments calling Muslims to jihad, to armed struggle, and to political violence. The symbolic arsenal appears medieval and obscurantist at the very least.

Will Islam evolve? The question appears to be a legitimate one, but its expression denotes another misunderstanding, the perpetuation of which today should itself be questioned as more or less deliberate. We must return to the source of the notion of jihad and seek a better understanding of its spiritual scope and dynamics. It is only through this understanding that we will be able to grasp the ways in which Islam does not negate the reality of potential conflicts – spiritual, as well as combative. Yet jihad remains first and foremost an act of resistance (to one's own excesses, as to oppression) and in all circumstances it is imperative that a number of conditions are respected in order to justify the said resistance. Moreover, at a global level, the struggle that Islam invites us to is that of the promotion of justice between nations, of social justice, of education and of the fight against poverty. It is a war against human excesses when humans forget themselves and spread exploitation, misery and persistent ignorance.

Chapter One

The seeds of violence

When dealing with issues related to war and peace, one cannot assume a merely circumstantial or event-specific reflection. For example, one might limit oneself to a topical reading of social or political events without returning to the sources of Islam – sources which must serve as distinct parameters from where theoretical thinking may be elaborated. Each Muslim and of course, non-Muslim, must thus be aware of what Islam says concerning these sensitive issues.

In the first instance, one must comprehend the Islamic concept of human beings and the universe, since one's concept of war is necessarily related to one's concept of these. If one believes that a human resembles angels, one need not discuss the topic of war. If on the other hand, one contends a human's bestial nature, one can imagine only war. Moreover, if one envisages a human who can be driven by both bestiality and can reach the highest degree of spirituality, the question becomes that of self-control and management of peace, as of war. It is clearly the latter concept which the Islamic sources of the Quran and Prophetic sayings describe.

Which 'violence'?

There is no Muslim living in the West who is not concerned by the issue of war and, more broadly, by the global situation. The current world order is indeed horrifying. Today, 40,000 people die of hunger every day, of which approximately 10,000 die due to debt. Never has a world order, well before the emergence of powerful technologies or globalisation, caused as many deaths as in the last two centuries, and more particularly in recent times. The calculations are simple: every two days, the current death toll is equivalent to the mortality caused by the Hiroshima bomb.[1] The reality of the world is that this 'violence' does not occur through weapons.

'Violent Muslims', a pleonasm

Exploitation, civil strife and poverty are an everyday reality, and yet these are not seen as real; instead weapons alone are viewed as the instruments of 'war'. In this sense, the West perceives the world of Islam as the most 'violent'.

In his famous article on the 'clash' of civilisations, Samuel Huntington[2] asserted that in all the areas bordering the western world, those with the highest level of conflict belong to the Islamic world, to Islamic civilisation. One cannot deny that in terms of frequency, there is an objective reality: armed violence occurs in many Muslim countries. Nonetheless, too often this fact is used to claim a link, implicitly akin to a rule, which then appears itself as evidence: violence is an intrinsic fact of Islam. The conclusion is clearly pernicious, but carries real weight today. In their way of presenting Islam, a number of journalists and researchers convey the idea that Islam is, by nature, violent.

We rediscover old ideas here – ideas which were dominant during the Middle Ages and which we thought had since been revoked; such as the idea that Islam was seen as hordes of marauding Muslims seeking to impose themselves, or convert people by the sword.

On this topic, we might recall the opinion of Chateaubriand[3] , one of the greatest French Christian thinkers who said: 'We should be thankful for the crusades which halted the possible expansion of the "mohamedans", continually seeking to impose their law.' We thought such discourse was outdated, but in fact, this same vision of the 'islamic danger', the 'green peril', is entrenched today.

In one of his works, Bat Ye'or[4] says precisely that; according to Islamic sources, and thus for Muslims, things are simple: there are two worlds; on one side are the Muslims and on the other, the non-Muslims. The Muslims are part of 'dar al Islam'(the world of Islam), and the non-Muslims are part of 'dar al harb'(the world of war) in which there are only two options: to convert, or devote oneself to seeking the application of the 'barbaric sharia'. As long as neither option is acted upon, Muslims will not be satisfied – because their religion will not have been thoroughly applied. What does this mean? Simply that the violence one witnesses in Muslim countries is derived from the very heart of Islam. What Bat Ye'or suggests to his readers is that by its very nature, Islam is a religion of conquest which legitimises the use of weaponry.

Clearly, this type of interpretation justifies perfunctory and particularly dangerous readings. Drawing on current world events which it claims as evidence that violence is indeed dominant, the theory appears to be verified: Islam is a violent religion; it is conquering and warmongering, and Muslims have only two concerns: to convert people or to impose themselves by any means, including the potential of terrorist acts. By extension, the underlying and insidious interpretation regarding the Israeli-Palestinian conflict is apparent: terrorism is necessarily one-sided and the Israeli state is merely defending itself.

Muslims can then attempt to deny the fact their religion does not incite them to war, that the violence we are witnessing does not emanate from Islam, that such simplifications are in fact inerrancies; but they can no longer limit themselves to superficial rejections. Their answers must draw on historical examples, just as they must also draw on the foundations of their faith.

Many intellectuals have a particularly vitiated understanding of the history of Islamic civilisation. While describing the expansion of Islam in the preface to the book by Bat Ye'or, a well-known personality such as Jacques Ellul[5] writes that it 'all occurred in blood'. The statement made is both serious and without nuance, in addition to which it is an untruth. Such a lack of objectivity in assessing history undoubtedly threatens our current relations.

It is imperative that we deepen our understanding of our own references in order to contribute a real and substantial clarity to these issues: firstly by drawing on our sources, then by truly comprehending the current world order. It is not about returning to the Quran arguing, 'You know, the Quran and the Prophet (s) encourage us to be peaceful, so everything you see today is not Islam.' This type of answer creates more problems than it actually resolves.

Unfortunately, we do not dedicate ourselves enough to providing a clear answer and yet do not cease to complain about the lack of one. And yet, we are the first to point the finger of blame for this state of affairs. Who else other than a Muslim should answer when criticisms are made of references that he/she identifies as his/her own? How many Muslims can answer calmly, clearly...sincerely? We hope this discourse will be a useful contribution to this end.

Chapter Two

Peace at the heart of Islam

What Muslims know, understand and experience of their religion is first and foremost its essential link with a feeling of peace, calm and deep serenity. The word 'islam' is the fourth grammatical form of the same root as salama: islam and aslama meaning to give oneself or dedicate oneself fully to God in the peace of one's heart: *'Truly it is in the remembrance of God that hearts find peace.' (Quran 13:28)*

To rely on God, to desire peace arduously through this closeness, the peace of 'the one who is close', this is what we aspire to with all our being. This is how, drawing on the example of our Prophet (s), we invoke the Most High: 'Oh God, You are Peace, from You comes Peace and it is from you that Peace returns.' Could there be any clearer aspirations of harmony? Furthermore, in our daily sayings, at the heart of what we learn, peace is primary and mercy a necessity. And yet, in all that we teach, in all that we say, this often fails to transpire. So infrequently do we demonstrate peace that people come to doubt its reality. Even we ourselves can effectively have doubts concerning the gentleness, the love and the sincere peace that Islam is meant to foster.

And yet, Islam is first and foremost this radiance; at the very moment we greet our brother or our sister, do we not say 'As-salam' alaykum wa rahmatullah wa barakatu-hu'? As-salam – peace. 'May the peace, the mercy and the blessings of God be with you.' This is our discourse, sometimes pronounced without thought, sometimes with fraternity and love. At the end of our prayers, those same words form our salutations – addressing the angels and all the beings around us, in the spirit of spreading this peace.

What is the object of all our desires? What do we hope for beyond this life? We all yearn for paradise, which revelation refers to through different names: 'aj-jannah', but also 'dar as-salam', the abode of peace.

> *'God invites [everyone] to the Home of Peace [...].'*
> *(Quran 10:25)*

If God calls us to the abode of peace, is it not correct therefore, to say that our teachings are essentially founded on the search for peace, as much internal as social? This is what we seek to translate daily in our interaction with God, with animals, with the environment, with human beings... not solely among Muslims:

> *'[Believers], argue only in the best way with the*

> *People of the Book, except with those of them who*
> *act unjustly [...].'*
>
> *(Quran 29:46)*

> *'Speak to him gently so that he may take heed, or*
> *show respect.'*
>
> *(Quran 20:44)*

Who must speak gently to whom? Moses and Aaron must speak thus to Pharaoh – the worst dictator, the model of pride and arrogance. This interaction of kindness and love is not limited to human beings, but extends to creation in its entirety. The man who quenched his thirst at a well and then saw a parched dog and saved it from dying: the prophetic tradition teaches us that paradise is promised to him. Whereas the woman who abused her cat until its death: she will receive the worst of punishments.

This general framework in Islamic teachings fills our hearts with compassion, our vocabulary draws its richness from it and yet we speak of it too little. We should repeat it constantly. The message of Islam is a message of love: essentially, fundamentally, at its very core.

This is what we must encourage of each other – to remind ourselves of patience and mercy:

> *'And to be one of those who believe and urge one*
> *another to steadfastness and compassion.'*
>
> *(Quran 90:17)*

Compassion is the promise of peace. And yet, it is not for Muslims to lock themselves away, hiding in a refuge of spirituality, occupied solely with the practice of worship in seeking total peace far from the affairs of this world, in absolute mysticism. On the contrary, we must face things and the first thing we must consider is the true nature of human beings. Are they constantly seeking peace? Are they really enamoured with serenity? Do they really love honesty and truth? Certainly not; and we needn't look very far for manifestations of conflict and adversity. Each of us must look within our inner self…what do we find?

Two explicit paths

Islam encourages peace, but which human could claim not to know within his or her inner core, feelings of violence? Sometimes aggression, sometimes hatred, sometimes the excitement of a destructive instinct, sometimes anger? Self control, serenity, respect for others, gentleness – these are only acquired through constant personal efforts. This is the lot of human beings: we reach the banks of our own humanity through protracted, reflective and measured work on ourselves. Everyone is aware of it, each heart feels it. It is due to our human nature. Within each of us, there are two orientations:

- the path of acceptance and obedience
- the path of refusal and negation

'Content is he who purifies his heart, miserable is he who perverts it.' The first evidence of this tension appears in our inner selves: each one of us has a desire, a strong desire, to purify his being and to give way to his spiritual aspirations. At the same time, we feel the weight of this solitary challenge: each of us is acutely aware of our capacity for violence, for getting carried away, the desire for wealth, fame and power. None can deny the reality of this inner tension: whoever denies this is claiming angelic status and he who claims to be an angel is close, according to Pascal's[6] famous saying, to becoming a beast. The Islamic sources enforce that sentiment: whoever believes they are pure is rendered impure through that belief alone. Perhaps the worst trait is that of pride (al-kibriya).

All literature, since the dawn of time, is full of the translation of this tension which at times subsides, at times resurfaces, tearing up human intimacy. From the Bhagavad-Gita[7] to the Torah[8] and the Gospels[9], from Dostoyevsky[10] to Baudelaire[11], the human horizon remains the same. The Quran confirms the most mundane of experiences:

> 'by the soul and how He formed it and inspired
> it [to know] its own rebellion and piety! The one
> who purifies his soul succeeds and the one who
> corrupts it fails.'
>
> *(Quran 91:7–10)*

The two paths are explicit and can be understood all the more vividly and morally in light of the remembrance of the h ereafter. Life is the challenge of balance for human-kind which is capable of the best, as of the worst.

A natural and human tension

We are now getting closer to the notion of jihad which can only be understood in light of the concept of the human being which underlies it. The tension is natural; the internal conflict is strictly human. We travel this path and become ever more human through our efforts to give strength and presence to the least violent, the least angry and the least aggressive inclinations of our being: we know that our own humanity will come at the price of mastering these. This intimate effort, this struggle between the 'postulations' of the inner-self is the most appropriate translation – both literal and figurative – of jihad.

This is not an attempt at reducing the meaning of jihad to the intimate and personal dimension (jihad an-nafs), but it is about bringing it back to its most immediate expression of reality: jihad is to human beings what instinct is to the behaviour of animals. For human beings, to be is to be responsible; and this responsibility is linked to choice, which should always seek to express kindness and respect for ourselves as well as for others. Choice is, within the context of an inner conflict, to resolve oneself to seek the peace of the heart.

There is a well-known saying of the Prophet (s), which is recognised as having a weak (da'if) chain of transmission, but from which we can draw a lesson given the extent to which other traditions confirm both its meaning and scope: Upon returning from an expedition where Muslims encountered their enemies, the Prophet (s) referred to war as the 'lesser jihad' compared with the 'greater jihad', the latter being the effort for internal purification and spiritualisation before the Creator. More than the comparison itself, what we must retain is the association of faith with the experience of efforts to attain harmony and serenity. Life is this struggle, and spiritual strength is indicated by the choice of good – of good actions for the self and for others:

> *'who created death and life to test you [people] and reveal which of you does best […].'*
>
> *(Quran 67:2)*

Reforming one's inner self, appeasing one's heart at the altar of recognition of the Creator, engaging in the mass of human and generous actions, to love in all transparency and to live in the light – this is the meaning of Islamic spirituality. It rejoins the horizon of all forms of spirituality which require humankind to equip themselves with a strength of being, rather than undergoing the despotic assault of a life reduced to instinct alone. The tension towards self-control is translated in Arabic by the word jihad. Understanding this dimension is the necessary first step towards a broader discussion of the meaning of armed conflict, which the term also encompasses. What must be remembered first and foremost, on the individual as on the collective level, it that God willed this tension and that He made the management of this tension one of the conditions of access to faith and humanity. It is an act of 'self-violence' when we face our basest and most negative inclinations, in order to accede to the dignity of self-control:

'The Prophet (s) asked one day: "Who is the strongest amongst you?" The companions responded, "The one who beats his enemy." The Prophet (s) responded, "The strong is not the one who overcomes the people by his strength. But the strong is the one who controls himself while in anger".' (Reported by Bukhari and Muslim)

Before we speak of international wars, we must speak first of these conflicts of the inner self: the believer – as is the lot of all humans – knows his inner tensions and knows the price of self-control. Our heart can become a battlefield; often, they are exactly that.

Chapter Three

The reality of conflicts

Humility requires us to recognise that within us there is an excess of violence, bouts of anger. The accomplished believer is not the one who never experiences internal conflicts, rather it is the one who, while recognising them, manages their passion and all that can lead them to war – internal and external.

Diversity is God's will

We mentioned previously that the Quran refers to diversity as an explicit choice of the Creator.

> *'[…] If God had so willed, He would have made you one community, but He wanted to test you through that which He has given you: so race to do good […].'*
>
> *(Quran 5:48)*

The role of diversity must be recognised: it is our challenge. When dealt with correctly, it equates to rivalry in kindness; but when mismanaged, it expresses itself through the desire for power and exploitation. What does the Quran tell us about this explicitly? From the earliest dawn of the earth, human beings have known adversity – it is our test. The best amongst us are those who will best know how to manage it, in dignity and with justice. The best amongst us are the most pious:

> '[…] the most honoured of you are the ones most
> mindful of Him […].'
>
> (Quran 49:13)

The most mindful are those who control their passions and succeed in working on themselves. Moreover, who is the best among nations? It is the community which succeeds best in working on itself, in self-regulating, in being more able to cope with adversity. Once more, to deny the reality of adversity while affirming that we are all good, all equal and so forth, as the background to the 'great idea' of pacifism, can lead us to the worst of consequences. When we deny reality, the naivety of these good intentions can lead to the creation of the most powerful dictatorships. Idealism, of the left or the right, whether it is communist, capitalist or mystical, has caused serious damage throughout history. We must confront reality and be discerning. God commands us to compete in kindness, to use diversity for good, to awaken in nations the spirit of positive emulation: for good, for peace, for respect. Elsewhere we find:

> *'People, We created you all from a single man and a single woman, and made you into races so that you should recognise one another [...].'*
>
> *(Quran 49:13)*

This verse is addressed to the whole of humanity and it provides the following direction: 'You are different, seek to know one another better. You are not the same as me, you don't have the same ideas as me, you don't have the same sensibility as me, but my task is to know you and to seek a respectful balance.' It is the same for nations and tribes. The purpose of diversity finds its meaning in the act of seeking to know one another. And yet diversity proves to be a challenge: the management of differences is presented as a test which must be met – in the same way, in fact, that each of us must meet the challenge of our inner tensions. The greatness of humankind depends on choice, and the Quran directs people through the aspiration 'race to do good'.

Seeking the balance of forces

At the same time, it must be noted that the balance between forces is a stabilising factor on this earth; this is an important concept in Islam. We find the following verse in the Quran:

> *'[…] If God did not drive some back by means of*
> *others, the earth would be completely corrupt: but*
> *God is bountiful to all.'*
>
> *(Quran 2:251)*

This verse is of great importance, it translates an idea of the world and of the relationships between humans: the balance of forces, in the form of the adversity which pits people and nations against one another, maintains the order of the world and of things. From the moment a majority of people are struggling for good, good will reign on earth. The opposite is equally true. Thus, if people did not oppose one another, with the according balance which flows from this, the earth would become depraved. In other words, if power, might, force had been concentrated once and for all, in the hands of a single person, of a single nation, of a single civilisation, our universe would have been destroyed. In brief: since diversity is the source of our challenge, the balance of forces is the exigency of our destiny.

Managing plurality

Another verse starts in the same fashion:

> *'[…] If God did not repel some people by means*
> *of others, many monasteries, churches, synagogues,*
> *and mosques, where God's name is much invoked,*
> *would have been destroyed […].'*
>
> *(Quran 22:40)*

We note with interest that monasteries, churches and synagogues are mentioned before mosques, and that it is very clearly an expression of their inviolability as well as the respect owed to the followers of different religions. The formulation couldn't be more explicit:

> *'Had your Lord willed, all the people on earth would have believed. So can you [Prophet] compel people to believe?'*
>
> *(Quran 10:99)*

Differences in religion, as with differences of colour and language, are facts with which we must coexist. It is worth recalling with emphasis here that the first principle of coexistence in diversity is that of respect and justice. Once again, the Quran is very clear:

> *'You who believe, be steadfast in your devotion to God and bear witnesses impartially: do not let hatred of others lead you away from justice, but adhere to justice, for that is closer to awareness of God: God is well aware of all that you do.'*
>
> *(Quran 5:8)*

The reality is stated: man is a conflictual being, a being who opposes others. In sum, the problem is not one of denying the fact of war; it is about knowing how to manage the reality of conflicts. Because it is possible to enter into conflict with others, because nothing is more human than this reality, because our daily existence is marked by an opposition between contradictory forces; for all of these reasons, we need rules of coexistence, which begin with mutual recognition and are completed through the application of justice and balance. This is the major teaching of Islam: human beings have the capacity to manage their internal balance, not by denying what they are, but by managing who they are. Since they can be the worst, they must strive to be the best.

Armed resistance is possible

As we are faced with inevitable conflicts of interest and the desire for power, the real testimony of faith lies in respecting each other's rights. If these rights are flouted and injustice spreads, it becomes the human's responsibility to oppose this state of affairs. It is precisely under such circumstances that the first verse was revealed, calling to jihad here in the context of armed resistance:

> *'Those who have been attacked are permitted to take up arms because they have been wronged – God has the power to help them – those who have been driven unjustly from their homes only for saying "Our Lord is God" [...].'*
>
> *(Quran 22:39–40)*

After suffering violent persecution for almost thirteen years in Mecca, and having to exile themselves to Medina, this verse allowed Muslims to defend themselves in the name of respect – for their faith and for justice. Abu Bakr, Muhammad's (s) companion, understood the scope of this message and stated that with this revelation: 'We understood that it meant armed struggle '. We find here an explicit expression of what jihad encompasses on both the inter-community and international level. Just as we had noted that the matter of struggling against forces of aggression is inherent to human beings on the personal level, it is also necessary here to note that resistance to every aggression and exploitation naturally occurs at a communal level, where fundamental rights are ignored.

Everything in the message of Islam calls to peace and coexistence among people and between nations. In all circumstances, one will favour dialogue to silence, and peace to war. To the exception of a specific situation in which fighting is a duty and resistance is a testimony of faith, jihad is the expression of the rejection of all injustice; it is the necessary affirmation of harmony in equity. While we might desire a non-violent struggle removed from the horror of weapons, and yearn for humankind to have the maturity of soul which would allow for a less bloody management of worldly affairs, we cannot deny history – a history that shows us humans are by nature bellicose, and that war is merely one means of expression.

Resistance to this overly violent expression while maintaining the necessary balance of forces, appear to be the conditions of a man-made order: this is the only case in which violence is legitimised. Pope John Paul II[12] took a stand on the situation in former Yugoslavia when he stated that military intervention is permissible if it is a case of defence against indignant aggression[13], as in the case of Bosnia. The same stance can be found from Abbé Pierre[14] of Sarajevo who called for the West's armed intervention basing himself on the example and teachings of Jesus.

In Islam therefore, there are situations where armed resistance is legitimate; particularly in situations where violence, repression, and the denial of rights are such that to submit to them would be to lose one's human dignity.

> 'God commands justice, doing good, and generosity towards relatives and He forbids what is shameful, blameworthy and oppressive [...].'
>
> (Quran 16:90)

The verse clearly expresses the nature of human actions: struggle for good and refuse injustice with all the strength of your being. To bear witness to faith is to bear witness to dignity through resistance. Resistance for the community is what self control at times of anger is to the inner self.

Chapter Four

The five conditions of resistance

War is something despicable and each of us, in our inner self, rejects it, but sometimes one must be resigned to it. We find in the Quran the expression of this tension. Revelation overlaps here with rational observation, in all its clarity:

> *'Fighting is ordained for you, though you dislike it.*
> *You may dislike something although it is good for*
> *you, and like something although it is bad for you:*
> *God knows and you do not.'*
>
> *(Quran 2:216)*

Revelation, in this sense, offers us a clear message: love others from the deepest depths of yourself, yet with the best application of your intelligence, be wary of them. Beware of what humans can be, because if they forget God and justice, they forget themselves. Whoever forgets themselves can destroy and kill for their own interest, for the love of money and power, whatever veneer they may coat their actions with. We observe this reality daily.

As Muslims, we must realise that we are called upon to take reality into account. We must understand our own nature and all that composes it – beautiful and the less than beautiful. We must always pursue peace, but also prepare ourselves for the struggle against injustices and oppression. In this sense, the duty of resistance is extremely important in Islam. Note, we are clearly saying resistance, and not compulsion or opposition.

If God had willed it, He would have made us all of the same religion; yet rather the human experience is about accepting the presence of the other, respecting their differences and remembering the Quranic teachings addressed to the Prophet (s):

> *'Had your Lord willed, all the people on earth*
> *would have believed – all who are on earth! So*
> *can you [Prophet] compel people to believe?'*
> *(Quran 10:99)*

Human justice is not absolute justice: the image of scales one finds above all the doors to courthouses the world over, expresses this search for balance. The Prophet (s) himself, in his judgements between individuals, always reminded people that he was a man and could make mistakes. We are all in search of the highest justice and we must expend our utmost energy in this pursuit.

We are touching on an essential question here: if injustices and thus conflicts are humanly possible, what are the criteria for their management? Plainly, what are the conditions which render war possible and confer legitimacy upon it? Since there are conditions (shurut) in Islam, we cannot wage war over just any objective. There exist motives which, by their expression alone, remove all legitimacy from war. A number of texts have been written on this topic where we find innumerable explanations by Muslim scholars (ulema) from the second century hijra until today. In light of these works, we can identify five conditions presented by the scholars concerning the legitimacy of war and jihad.

War as a system of defence

The first verse concerning war was revealed, according to the sayings of Abu Bakr and other companions, during the second year of the hijra. This is, in and of itself, very instructive: during the persecution that the Muslims underwent in Mecca, it was a matter not of war, but rather of resistance, of faith (iman) in the reverential recognition of God (taqwa), of personal efforts (jihad an-nafs), of perseverance in the midst of an ordeal. Once settled in Medina, the Muslims heard these words:

> *'Those who have been attacked are permitted to take up arms because they have been wronged – God has the power to help them.'*
>
> *(Quran 22:39)*

Who does this verse refer to? It refers to the Prophet (s) and to his companions who had to face a new set of ordeals. As mentioned earlier, Abu Bakr affirmed: 'We understood that it meant armed struggle .' The Muslims had not experienced war during the first thirteen years of the revelation. The meaning of the verse as well as the circumstances of its revelation (sabab an-nuzul) leads us to state that the first situation which authorises Muslims to wage war is that of legitimate defence. It is permitted for them to react and defend themselves when they are unjustly attacked. It is the first verse revealed to Muslims in this sense (Quran 22:39), and it is clearly stipulated that it is possible to resist (Quran 22:41–42). It was a matter, at that time, of the survival of the first community of believers.

> 'Those who have been driven unjustly from their homes only for saying, "Our Lord is God." [...] those who, when We establish them in the land, keep up the prayer, pay the prescribed alms, command what is right, and forbid what is wrong: God controls the outcome of all events.'
>
> (Quran 22:40–41)

Another verse also refers to legitimate defence:

> 'Fight in God's cause against those who fight you, but do not overstep the limits: God does not love those who overstep the limits.'
>
> (Quran 2:190)

From this perspective, it is once again the case of legitimate defence which is permissible in Islam – it is the primary condition that allows struggle. Through this clarification, we can suggest a general theory on the topic of legitimate defence, but it is not of much use. In fact, one must analyse each situation on a case by case basis and must undertake a critical and circumstantial reflection. Issues are sometimes obvious, sometimes complex; while this may vary, the principle of legitimate defence remains clear.

The Prophet (s) said:

'He who dies in defence of his money, his country, his family or in defence of his religion or possessions, is considered a martyr.' (Hadith reported by An-Nassa'i)

It is therefore not simply a question of faith. The Prophet (s) refers to legitimate defence in all domains where an assault, theft or oppression can occur. A man came to see the Prophet (s) and said to him, 'Such and such person stole from me, what should I do?' The Prophet (s) responded to him:

'Ask by God that he return it to you.'
'And if he refuses?'
'Ask by God that he return it to you.'
'And if he refuses?'
Ask by God that he return it to you.'

'And if he refuses?'
'Then fight for it (your possession)!'

After the patient exhortation – just as the resistance of the Muslims was patient in the face of Meccan injustice – after the recommendation of words of peace, when there is no other option, then entering into war is legitimate in the defence of one's religion, life and possessions.

There is nothing here which is not rationally obvious, and we understand through these verses and these sayings the concept of a human being within Islam. One must learn to resist the violent, aggressive and unjust outbursts of human beings. Here, resistance is a factor creating balance between people, Muslim or not.

'The Prophet (s) said: "Help your brother whether he is oppressor or oppressed," Anas replied to him, "O Messenger of God, a man who is oppressed I am ready to help, but how does one help an oppressor?" "By hindering him doing wrong", he said.' (Hadith reported by al-Bukhari)

The sayings are clear and should awaken within us a worthy and vigilant conscience by insisting on justice for and from all, Muslim or not. The 'word of truth' (kalimat-al-haq) must be said, even if it is bitter. This is the meaning of another hadith which states: 'The best jihad is a word of truth spoken to an unjust ruler .'

Freedom of religion
The second condition is more specific than the first and is

expressed through the idea of defending freedom of faith, conscience and worship. This important condition is reflected upon in the following verses:

> *'Fight them until there is no more persecution, and*
> *worship is devoted to God. If they cease hostilities, there*
> *can be no [further] hostility, except towards aggressors.'*
> *(Quran 2:193)*

If someone is denied the freedom of practising their religion and persecuted for their faith, they must resist. However this does not mean they may reach for arms to 'implement justice'. For example, it should not be comprehended that in certain European countries 'they' don't want mosques, headscarves, or Muslim graveyards; 'they' are therefore opposed to my freedom of worship. This reasoning is erroneous and unfounded: for the majority of countries in the West, Muslims may practise their religion. Yes, there are some very specific points on which negotiations are currently underway, yet it is necessary to enter into dialogue and to move forward in consultation. Here is another verse which must serve to guide those of us living in the West:

> *"He does not forbid you to deal kindly and justly*
> *with anyone who has not fought you for your faith*
> *or driven you out of your homes: God loves the just.'*
> *(Quran 60:8)*

Aside from that which occurred in Bosnia, Kosovo or still today in the former Russian republics (crimes against humanity which must be denounced unequivocally), Muslims are not persecuted because of their religion in Europe. Wherever possible, it is necessary to establish open, respectful and friendly relations with those around us to increase mutual understanding.

If a man or a woman is obviously persecuted for his or her religion, he or she has the right to resist. This resistance should be relative to the oppression or persecution being faced: weapons are the last recourse if all other routes are inoperable, and where there is a total denial of rights and/ or we are suffering under an unjust and eradicating regime. Muslims must then react and resist. The remainder of the preceding verse states:

> 'But God forbids you to take as allies those who
> have fought against you for your faith, driven
> you out of your homes, and helped others to
> drive you out [...].'
>
> (Quran 60:9)

Henceforth, we are better able to understand the general message of Islam. Once more, we are invited to manage our anger and to determine ways of living together on the basis of respect for rights.

Freedom of expression

The third condition is related to freedom of expression. During the years following the Treaty of Hudaybiyya[15] (Sulh al-Hudaybiyya) between 628 and the death of the Prophet (s) in 632, Muhammad (s) sent emissaries to the leaders of all the great neighbouring empires. Why did he choose this moment? Because, peace having returned, it was possible for him to accomplish his primary mission: to make known his message.

Each person must be given the right of practising their religion and to speak of it freely, to present it or to explain it. This is the fundamental and inalienable right to freedom of expression from which everyone must be able to benefit.

Within the framework of the current reflection which concerns legitimate cases for war, we think and believe deeply, as Muslims, that the Quran is the last revelation sent to the whole of humanity. Such is the meaning of the passage:

> *'We have sent you [Prophet] only to bring good*
> *news and warning to all people, but most of them*
> *do not understand.'*
>
> *(Quran 34:28)*

Considering himself a messenger for the whole world in light of the revelation, the Prophet (s) sent at least nine delegates in five years, according to Ibn Hisham, to the populations of the neighbouring countries who knew nothing of Islam, or whose leaders were unaware of the reality of the new religion, and founded their judgements on vague conjecture.

In two famous cases, the attitude of the leaders towards the messengers of the Prophet (s) provoked wars, which was neither the objective of the delegation nor the rule governing relations with neighbouring nations. A war occurred first against the Byzantines, because the messenger of the Prophet (s), Harith Ibn Umayr, was killed by Amr al-Ghassani, one of the ministers of the Empire. A second conflict occurred against the Persians, when their leader tore up the Quran in front of the messenger and requested that his soldiers bring him back 'this Muhammad alive'. These two reactions were understood by the Muslims as declarations of war, whereas in almost all the other cases, the message was able to be transmitted without war or coercion. The priority was clearly to transmit the message of Islam to the populations. The leaders, at that time, were the immediate means through which to achieve this objective, because Islam is first a message 'for the people' (li n-nas) according to the Quranic saying, before being a guidance addressed to the authorities.

Today, our intimate connection to this universal message renders necessary the condition of being able to testify. This corresponds currently to what we refer to as 'freedom of expression'. He who, weapons in hand, desires to impose silence on us while affirming 'you do not have the right to testify to your religion' infringes a fundamental right which comes from freedom of expression. This right must be guaranteed to us just as we must guarantee it to others: with respect for other people's convictions, everyone has a right to express themselves freely, Muslim or not.

It is therefore necessary to resist any person, wherever and whoever they may be, who says: 'You cannot state who you are, you do not have the right to express your faith and your opinions.' Of course, peace is our most ardent desire; but if we are fought, we would have to clearly manifest our duty to resist. It must be no less evident than the fact that testifying to one's religion does not mean forcing people to embrace the Muslim religion:

> *'There is no compulsion in religion: true guidance has become distinct from error, so whoever rejects false gods and believes in God has grasped the firmest hand-hold, one that will never break. God is all hearing and all knowing.'*
>
> *(Quran 2:256)*

Indeed, before a contextualised definition, the first fundamental rule relative to relations between Muslims and non-Muslims was assessed on the basis of the actions of the Prophet (s) as being a 'state of peace' and not a 'state of war'. The second is that the Prophet (s), above all else, wanted to address the people, not take power. The tradition shows that he always decided to combat leaders for murders they committed, their betrayals, or their injustices; he never fought any population because it chose not to convert to Islam. He wanted these leaders to choose while being fully aware of the message of Islam. After this, he accepted their choices and recognised their right to remain where they lived and to practise their religion. Non-Muslim populations paid a tax (jizya) in exchange for state protection. We know this fact and must try to apply and understand all the implications of the duty not to coerce.

Finally, to be free to express oneself does not imply that one has the right to say anything and everything: freedom of expression must be respectful of dignity, integrity, and religion as it must be of people's origins.

Respecting pacts

The Prophet (s) established certain pacts, the respect of which is presented as fundamental in the Quran. Whoever betrays a pact – as was the case with certain tribes who violated the agreement established with the community of Medina – commits one of the most serious offences. It is undoubtedly a matter of high treason and, in this case, the pact is broken. Permission is thus given to the Muslims to enter into war against those who breached their pacts. This is what the Prophet (s) had to do many times, in particular following the Treaty of Hudaybiyya, at the moment of entry into Mecca.

The sayings of the Quran are clear:

'But if they break their oath after having made an agreement with you, if they revile your religion, then fight the leaders of disbelief – oaths mean nothing to them – so that they may stop.'

(Quran 9:12)

The other verse is well known:

'[…] Honour your pledges: you will be questioned about your pledges.'

(Quran 17:34)

The duty of solidarity

If an oppressed Muslim calls upon another Muslim, the latter must respond to the first, in any way they can:

'[…] if they seek help from you against persecution, it is your duty to assist them, except against people with whom you have a treaty. God sees all that you do.'

(Quran 8:72)

The Quran invites us to recognise a sizeable objective truth: the restriction concerning respect of an agreement. If we expect others to honour agreements, we owe it to ourselves to honour them in the same way; they cannot be betrayed. After Hudaybiyya, the Prophet (s) respected the content of the agreement through which he was bound to the Quraysh: he was unable to protect a fleeing Muslim because the clauses of the contract forbade him from doing so, thus he was forced to send him back. It was only after the Quraysh's betrayal that he intervened – the clauses were now void.

These five situations provide an understanding of the cases in which resistance and war are legitimate in Islam. What can we deduce from this? We deduce that war can be justified when it is a matter of defending justice. The latter does not emerge naturally by itself; it requires that people of faith, of good and with good will, resist antagonistic forces that seek power, exploitation and force. These conditions render clear the duty of every Muslim: to engage in good and resist evil and violence – within oneself, as in society.

Chapter Five

Five principles – what are the lessons learned?

From the five principles, or conditions, laid out above, it is possible to extract a number of teachings concerning the management of peace and war in Islam.

The priority of justice

These reflections offer us firstly a concept of the universe and of humankind: diversity exists and is a challenge. Within this challenge, doing good lies in resisting all injustices. We perceive here a clear message to all Muslim men and women: in front of God – justice comes first! If God inhabits the hearts of the believers and if it is in light of His reminder the way they live their lives, then justice will be their companion and it must, in all circumstances, bear witness to their actions. None should become the accomplice of injustice either actively or passively, or out of negligence. Allowing unjust actions to occur is akin to participating in them, to being an accomplice to them.

On the contrary, driven by their faith, Muslims ought to be the greatest resisters to the shameless exploitation and unjust disorder of this world. Armed with good will, all Muslims must be the carriers of the greatest exigency of justice by firmly opposing all types of oppression.

In the West, in the same way, social and political justice must be a priority: whoever the person suffering injustice might be, an injustice is one injustice too many. Our faith forbids us from accepting injustice and it must be denounced with one's voice, one's intellect and one's heart.

As for weapons and war, we have seen the precise conditions relating to their use; and only an analysis on the ground, with a serious and circumstantial evaluation of all the avenues permitting the avoidance of armed conflict, will allow us to know if – as a last resort – we need to arrive at this level of resistance.

Struggling for supremacy motivated by a desire for power; struggling to conquer land which does not belong to us in order to acquire mineral resources or simply for prestige, is categorically forbidden in Islam. It couldn't be clearer.

Seeking only peace
Secondly, we must realise that peace, using the means of justice, must be the objective of all actions of resistance.

It is said:

> *'You who believe, enter wholeheartedly into submission to God and do not follow in Satan's footsteps, for he is your sworn enemy.'*
>
> (Quran 2:208)

In all our enterprises, in all our undertakings, we must first seek and desire peace. Some may speak of jihad and of death with worrying ease; killing, taking away the life of a man or woman is not an insignificant action. War, as such, is a serious and difficult issue that we cannot discuss lightly. We must remember what is said to us:

> *'On account of [his deed], We decreed to the Children of Israel that if anyone kills a person – unless in retribution for murder or for spreading corruption in the land – it is as if he kills all mankind [...].'*
>
> (Quran 5:32)

Killing someone is like killing the whole of humankind if it is done in an act of injustice. We must be wary of this easy discourse in the West, in front of one's television set, that we can kill and that nothing is more normal. The five principles suggest that this is not the case: woe to the one who engages in a discourse encouraging war, the consequences of which they do not know. One must be mindful and understand the responsibility of a person to defend life. The following part of the verse is clear on this issue:

> *'[...] if any saves a life it is as if he saves the lives of all mankind [...].'*
>
> *(Quran 5:32)*

In addition, the following verse is also clear:

> *'But if they incline towards peace, you [Prophet] must also incline towards it [...].'*
>
> *(Quran 8:61)*

It is not a case of desiring war, quite the contrary. And this is precisely what the Prophet (s) was told: we must always seek out peace while remaining rigorous in our search for justice. It cannot be a case of peace in name only, or a peace which might be founded on an injustice. Peace is not a mere word that we use out of expediency; peace has its rules, and they must be respected, whether they are in our favour or not.

It is essential that we undertake the effort to explain this because throughout the world some Muslims confirm, through their behaviour, the view that Islam is a religion of war or hatred. Yet we have just stated that Islam requires resistance in front of God – for justice, with determination, unequivocally. We have repeated the fact that Islam enjoins us to seek out peace; but there is no peace without justice. Peace without justice is not peace; at best, it is an advertising poster, a sophism or...a soporific.

At the heart of war

It must be acknowledged that unfortunately, humans are capable of the worst acts. In Islam, there are rules, even in war: the sentiment of 'anything goes' during war is not acceptable. When the Prophet (s) sent a troop to an expedition, he would say to them: 'Place your trust in God. Go in the name of God. Do not betray anyone, do not behave like them.' These were his prescriptions.

The precise sayings of Abu Bakr echoed the teachings of the Prophet (s). When Abu Bakr sent the young Usama on an expedition to Syria, he defined the big moral and humanitarian principles of Islam, giving the following directives:

'Trust in God; you will not harm the elderly, nor the children, nor the women. You will not attack them nor will you harm them. You will not uproot the fruit trees. As for those who sought refuge in a place of worship, you will leave them in peace. There is an enemy: that enemy is armed. Women, children, the elderly and men of religion – you will spare. '

Such is the attitude recommended during war: one must be dignified, noble and not attack those who are not directly implicated in the conflict. The principle is derived from an injunction: avoid war; yet if due to circumstances you are obliged to engage in it, restrict yourself to the absolute necessary. In all situations, avoid excess and do not fight those who do not fight you directly.

We can therefore highlight three moral and humanitarian principles which must motivate the conflict:

1. Defend and promote justice;
2. Seek to establish peace among people;
3. Strike only those directly implicated in the conflict, never the innocent, nor nature.

The Prophet (s) always behaved according to these principles, never veering away from Islamic teachings. If he condemned and fought betrayal, it was always with dignity and nobleness. These principles, which are worth analysing in more depth, offer us a frame of reference concerning the general context. It is necessary to be vigilant and not blindly trust people's intentions. We must protect ourselves against negative penchants, excesses and violence – in oneself, as in others. Sometimes we slip into inconsiderate and hurtful speech, even though we are warned against it. There is a verse which all Muslims ought to know – words we must heed from the pinnacle of the seven heavens:

> *'You who believe, be steadfast in your devotion*
> *to God and bear witness impartially: do not let*

hatred of others lead you away from justice, but adhere to justice, for that is closer to awareness of God. Be mindful of God: God is well aware of all that you do.'

(Quran 5:8)

In a situation of war, at the moment of confrontation, the individual may feel hatred developing inside him: when he sees what men are capable of doing, the unlimited manifestations of violence...all of this can lead to blindness. And yet, we must control ourselves, through a conscience reinvigorated before God, so as not to become unjust: 'adhere to justice, for that is closer to awareness of God.'

Other verses regarding war

There are other verses in the Quran (and they are numerous, notably in chapter nine entitled 'Repentance', the only one which does not begin with Bismillah ar-Rahman ar-Rahim) which could give the impression of legitimating violence and war. If they were read literally, it would become possible to combat and kill all those who are not like us and who are not Muslim.

From the beginning of exegesis, scholars who codify Islamic prescriptions have highlighted the fact that revelation was elaborated over twenty-three years and that the significance of numerous verses must be contextualised. In this sense, the absolute character of the revealed rule is not in the literal understanding of the text, but in a profound understanding of the revelation – between the meaning of the verse and the context of revelation (sabab an-nuzul). This placing into perspective is crucial and inevitable: the particular verses, specifically relating to a particular context, must be understood in light of the latter and cannot express the general teachings of Islam. These general teachings, which we have presented in this discourse, contain principles which are found throughout classical scholarship on this topic. It is in light of these teachings that one must read the other verses relating to war and give them a contextual scope and not an absolute one. A revealed verse or hadith concerning a case of legitimate defence at the time of the Prophet (s) cannot be used today to justify aggression, or the murder of Jews, Christians or atheists for the sole reason that they are Jews, Christians or atheist.

Terrorism

We have heard from some 'scholars' and Muslim leaders who, from a literalist and truncated reading, call to a jihad of which none or very few of its conditions are actually respected. From their discourse emanates the idea that blind, armed struggle is legitimate and that no non-Muslim is truly 'innocent'. In the war against the 'American oppressor' or 'colonising Zionism', it seems that anything goes. This is indeed what we heard here and there after the attacks of September 11th 2001 in the United States.

Some sought to avoid the question by stating that according to the facts, we could not determine who had organised these attacks. That the definitive proofs were lacking, is a fact. Yet it is an equally undeniable fact that there are Muslims (including Bin Laden himself who said and wrote as much) who think that you can spread violence and kill non-Muslims and the kuffar (the deniers), for the mere fact they are non-Muslim. We must state and emphasise here that these sayings do not respect the principles of Islam, and that they betray its general teachings.

In this sense, condemnation of terrorist acts like those which occurred in New York must be unequivocal. Nothing in Islam can legitimate these actions.

However we must be wary of not falling into simplistic analogies such as those which were made by the Israeli government when it affirmed, through Ariel Sharon, that Palestinian resistance is terrorism. Palestinian resistance is legitimate, as much in terms of international law as in light of Islamic teachings: Zionist occupation is colonisation, an aggression which translates as the systematic oppression of an entire people.

We must discuss the methods used, affirming that targeting civilians is not legitimate. For years, Palestinian resistance did not attack civilian targets but, with the continued oppression of the forces of Israeli occupation, the massive imbalance of power and the silence of the international community, their last recourse has been operations against civilians. We must condemn these actions just as one must condemn the attitudes of those parties involved in the management of this crisis. One simply cannot place all the blame on those men and women who are rejected, oppressed and whose only recourse is sacrificing their lives by attacking the only target they can reach (given the incredible Israeli military arsenal), while omitting to condemn Israeli politics – the primary producer of this violence. This in addition to criticising the unacceptable passivity of the United States and Europe in their treatment of the crisis, which offers moral impunity to the Israeli state's terrorism, and pushes the Palestinians towards the ultimate recourse of operations in order merely to be heard.

Sacrificing one's life

Much has been written about the 'martyr' and its supposed 'cult' in Islam. In light of our writings, the issues are clearer: resisting in the name of one's faith and one's conscience against all oppressions, all dictators and unjust colonisers, to the point of sacrificing one's own life if necessary, is a recommendation backed by the Quranic message. It is not about romanticising resistance, nor about a cult of the martyr, but it clearly concerns the meaning given to life as a testimony, for each and every one of us, of the values we carry: whoever dies in the struggle for resistance is named 'shahid', literally in Arabic, he/she 'bears testimony '.

Is this to say that in the name of the possible sacrifice of one's life for one's faith and conscience, one may behave in any which way? No, absolutely not; and the conditions that we have mentioned remain the rule, in addition to the requirement that those who engage in this are free and responsible. Children cannot be exposed to the exigencies of this sacrifice. Once more, one must beware of simplifications and lies which, in Palestine, claim that Palestinians expose their children in such a manner in order to draw emotion from international opinion and, in addition, that they perceive the value of their lives as less important. Even while oppressed, are they not still human?! Anyone who has visited the territories knows that the young teenagers who throw stones are not indoctrinated, and that children are not put on display. The reality is completely different: having their patience tested to the limit, their dignity flouted, their future deprived under the watch of an arrogant occupier – the youth are prepared to sacrifice their own lives. The roles must not be reversed, making the Israeli military out to be victims of those they oppress. Their actions, seen from any angle, are illegitimate.

Perhaps one day we will answer the question rightly formulated by a Palestinian academic: 'Instead of saying that Palestinians inhumanly expose their children, tell us with what humanity the soldiers who are taught to shoot at them are trained?' It is evident that discussing principles alone is not sufficient to understand specific situations. Yet it helps nonetheless to have a general clarification which allows us to nuance the simplistic discourse of individuals, Muslim or not.

Chapter Six

For a social jihad

We have spoken a great deal about peace and war, and have thus specified the central notion of jihad. We have insisted on the fact that there is no peace without justice. If we observe the world today, we see that the potential of war may breed wherever injustice occurs. We have stated that peace is constructed gradually, little by little, at the heart of society. Today, what we really need is a social jihad.

The multiple actions of jihad

All Muslims know that the practice of Islam does not stop at prayer, nor at the purifying tax, fasting or pilgrimage. Every action of daily life undertaken with the consciousness of the divine essence is, in itself, an act of gratefulness and adoration ('ibada). We also know of the firm link established in the Quran between belief and action, through the insistent repetition of the formula: 'Those who believe and do good deeds.' Hence, to bear witness is to believe and act – and action here has a pluralistic nature: it is as much the honesty that we abide by, the kindness and generosity towards one's relatives, as it is the determined engagement in social reforms, or the mobilisation against injustices. All these efforts deployed in action contribute to the meaning of jihad in the sense that they are directed towards a more just system and are more respectful of the revealed principles. The verse specifies:

> *'The true believers are the ones who have faith in God and His Messenger and leave all doubt behind, the ones who have struggled with their possessions and their persons in God's way: they are the ones who are true.'*

> *(Quran 49:15)*

One could read this verse in the literal sense and affirm that it refers to armed struggle, as mentioned earlier, which becomes an obligation when aggression occurs. This reading is supported by the context of the revelation of this verse, but it would be simplistic to draw from it this single teaching. In a broader sense, which is confirmed by the totality of the Quranic message and traditions, 'to struggle on the path of God' means mobilising all human forces, to direct all one's efforts, to give oneself and one's possessions in order to end all the adversities of injustice, poverty, illiteracy, crime and exclusion.

The Quran provides this latitude in the interpretation of the word jihad and this, from its earliest revelation:

> *'so do not give in to the disbelievers: strive hard against them with this Qur'an.'*
>
> *(Quran 25:52)*

Mentioned here is an understanding of struggle, jahid and jihadan, which is of an intellectual, scientific nature based on dialogue, discussion and debate: the Quran, in both its form and content, appears as a weapon in the hands of Muslims. On another front, the Prophet (s) himself presented an extensive explanation of the term when he affirmed, for example, that 'the pilgrimage is a jihad'. We gather from this that the efforts and suffering endured by the faithful during their days in Mecca when they respond to the call of their Creator, are a jihad on the path of God.

New challenges of the modern era

In our daily life, in our societies, living with faith is to acknowledge the meaning of struggle. Faith is being tested, faith is a test. Alongside our pursuit of an ideal life imbued with respect and coexistence, the modern era continues to foster adversities to a great extent: social fractures, misery, illiteracy, unemployment.

Mobilisation is necessary, as we have stated, when human dignity is in peril; but it is not always a matter of a call to arms. Today, too many people have their dignity flouted, their existence denied, their rights violated, and this situation requires an urgent response to a general call to jihad: it is a matter of giving one's self and one's possessions, to call on all the forces of diverse societies and to undertake efforts of reform mentioned previously.

We do not deny that there are struggles which circumstances will lead us to confront with weapons or stones in hand, in order to oppose ethnic cleansing, military occupation, or other types of aggression like that which we continue to witness in Afghanistan, Palestine, Chechnya or elsewhere. But it cannot be a case of focusing our attention on these events and forgetting a broader type of combat, more daily, and so very urgent.

Our enemies, today, in the path of God, can be identified as hunger, unemployment, exploitation, crime and drug addiction; and they require an intense effort, a continuous struggle – a total jihad from each and every one of us. How many Muslims want to fight 'over there', want to offer themselves up, in a most sincere fashion, for the cause of Islam, and who, filled with this intention, forget or remain blind to the struggle that must be waged here, to the causes which must be defended in one's neighbourhood, in one's city, in one's country? This jihad is a jihad for God and for life, so that each person can benefit from their rights: the entirety of the message of Islam carries this exigency at the same time as its necessary realisation.

This is a case of war. We are at war. This is the meaning of Father Pierre's words when he said with conviction: 'I am at war with misery', or moreover, the calls of Professor Albert Jacquard[16] and of Bishop Jacques Gaillot[17] when they 'went to war' against homelessness. Pope John Paul II, in his social encyclical[18] *Centesimus Annus* (1991), called for a general mobilisation against poverty and the imbalance in the distribution of wealth, and he affirmed that it is the duty of all Christians to act upon this.

The Muslim jihad falls within this involvement in the West of course, but also elsewhere: it is in complete accordance with the understanding of Latin American grassroots and the expression of the theology of liberation found therein; and with popular or trade union forces in the Middle East or Asia – where jihad is married to the message of the very demanding and dignified oriental spirituality. The future of inter-religious dialogue is fully realised in these types of strategies and concerted, concrete actions.

The promotion of 'legitimate violence' from the self to the management of conflicts, and the promotion of a commitment against our sectarian, aggressive and selfish tendencies reminds us that dignity and respect are not a state of mind which we adhere to out of a mere kindness of the heart; they constitute ideals which require a full investment of our energies – internally and collectively – in the rediscovery of the 'meaning of effort' and of the 'imperative of resistance'.

There is no peace without effort, without exigency, without resistance. Human acts remind us of this so often… our heart often tells us as much. Non-violence is not a state of being, but a path: in society it requires a profound education; at an individual level, an initiation.

Conclusion

Today, we note effervescence in the Muslim world and many condemn the violence which accompanies the awakening of a 'fanatical, radical and fundamentalist Islam'. We must understand this concern and we must denounce the political violence which is expressed through the assassination of tourists, priests, women and children, through blind bombings and bloody carnage. These actions cannot be defended and in no way respect the Quranic message.

In addition, we must condemn the violence expressed previously – the consequence of dictatorial powers which are all too often supported by superpowers. Every day that passes, entire peoples are subject to repression, the abuse of power, and the most inhumane violation of their rights. How long must they remain silent and be judged as 'dangerous' by the West while it refuses to oppose their subjugation?

It is not a matter of justifying violence, but it is a matter of comprehending under what circumstances violence comes about. Social imbalance, the exploitation of people and natural resources, together with the acquiescence of certain superpowers, creates violence more devastating still than the shocking display of armed groups. Can we call on people to mobilise for more justice, as much social as political and economic, because it appears to us as the only means of giving humans the rights which will lead them to lay down their weapons? This effort would be the literal translation of the word jihad... it is the testimony of a heart driven by faith and of a conscience shaped by responsibility.

After the September 11th attacks, in light of the attacks on the Afghan people, faced with the violence in Palestine and the atrocities committed in Chechnya and more broadly throughout the world in Tibet, China, and Indonesia, we cannot maintain a moralising and pacifying discourse. It is against the causes of violence and of war which we must struggle: firstly, by engaging in respective efforts at self-criticism, then by getting involved in the struggle for the rights of all peoples through a process of democratisation, which respects the choices of men and women throughout the world. We must also follow through with the logic of pluralism and accept diversity as certainly a risk when it comes to living together, but crucially as a condition of balance and harmony, avoiding the supremacy of any single person, or of any single power. The world needs other poles to emerge in the face of the American superpower: Europe must awaken, and throughout the world so must all forces of resistance, for the respect of the citizens of the world, for their freedom and for justice.

Endnotes

1. Hiroshima: Japanese town (Honshu), on the inner sea. The Americans dropped the first atomic bomb there on 6th August 1945, which killed approximately 140,000 people.

2. Huntington, Samuel (1927–2008): Political scientist at Harvard University who predicted in 1993 that international politics would be dominated by a 'clash of civilisations' opposing western culture to other cultures, notably that of the Muslim world.

3. Chateaubriand, François René (1768–1848): Viscount and French writer, most notably of *Genius of Christianity* (1802), where he sought to contribute to the restoration of moral order; of *René* (1805), in which *René* represents the 'ills of the century'; of *Memories from Beyond the Grave* (1848–1850), the writing of which took thirty years and which represents a meditation on history, time and death.

4. Bat Ye'or (born 1933): Pseudonym of Gisèle Littman, an Egyptian-born British author, notably of *The Dhimmi:-Jews and Christians under Islam'* and of *The Decline of Eastern Christianity under Islam: From Jihad to Dhimmitude* charting between the seventh and twentieth centuries.

5. Ellul, Jacques (1912–1994): French historian and member of the Reformed Church and the World Council of Churches. His work highlights his own interest in the increasing role of technology in contemporary society, as well as the place of propaganda and violence in modern life. Author of, most notably, *Propagandas* (1962), *The Technical System* (1977), *The Raison-d'être* (1987).

6. Pascal, Blaise (1623–1662): French mathematician, scientist and Catholic philosopher.

7. Bhagavad-Gita: 'Song of the Divine Lord', the most famous section of *Mahabharata,* a highly venerated Hindu text. Composed of eighteen chapters with seven hundred verses, this text is a veritable summary of the ideas of Hindu spirituality.

8. Torah: Name given in Judaism to the first five books of the Bible, or Pentateuch, which contains the essentials of Moses' law. In current parlance, it designates the totality of Jewish law.

9. The Gospels: Writings of the New Testament where the life and message of Jesus are described. Four in total, they are attributed to Matthew, Mark, Luke and John. Their writing is approximately dated between the years 70 and 80 for Matthew, Mark and Luke, and the year 100 for John.

10. Dostoyevsky, Fyodor Mikhaylovich (1821–1881): Russian writer, best known for *Crime and Punishment* (1866), *The Idiot* (1868), and *The Brothers Karamazov* (1879–1880).

11. Baudelaire, Charles (1821–1867): French poet and author notably of *Flowers of Evil* (1857).

12. John-Paul II, Karol Wojtyla (1920–2005): Pope since 1978, he opened the Roman Church to broad horizons, exercising a universal pastoral ministry (he travelled to all continents). He dedicated himself to struggling for social justice and defending human dignity.

13. *World Hunger and Humanity's Conscience*, 1992.

14. Father Pierre Henri Grouès, known as 'Abbé Pierre' (1912–2007): French priest who founded the Association Emmaüs in 1949, dedicated to helping the homeless. He devoted his life to the defence of the disinherited.

15. The treaty of Hudaybiyya was agreed near Mecca in 628 between Prophet Muhammad (s) and the leading representatives of his enemies who remained pagan, including the Qurayshi Abu Sufyan. The treaty included a ten year ceasefire, and permitted the Muslims to undertake the pilgrimage the following year during which the Quraysh would vacate Mecca for three days to accommodate the Muslim pilgrims. Two thousand Muslims came to perform the pilgrimage with the Prophet (s). The event had many effects: the desert tribes had seen the Meccans dealing with the Prophet (s) on an equal basis and as a leader, which led to many embracing Islam. Two months later, in 630, following an incident between an allied tribe and the Meccans declaring the ceasefire over, the Prophet (s) marched on Mecca and conquered it, encountering almost no resistance.

16. Jacquard, Albert (born 1925): French geneticist. Author most notably of *Praise of Difference: Genetics and Human Affairs* (1978). From this thinking came his struggle against racism and exclusion and his defence of the homeless.

17. Gaillot, Jacques (born 1935): Ordained a priest in 1961, Bishop of Evreux in 1982, he joined the cause of the homeless and notably published *Diatribe Against Exclusion* (1994). Following a conflict with the Vatican, he is named incumbent Bishop of Partenia.

18.   Encyclical: Letter solemnly addressed by the pope to the bishops and by them to the faithful, to the whole world, or to a region. It is referred to by its first two words in Latin.

Quranic references

The Qur'an: A New Translation, M.A.S Abdel Haleem, Oxford University Press, 2005